Zany Girl

Answers your natural hair questions

Tambeara Watkins

Copyright © 2016 by **Tambeara Watkins**

All rights reserved. No part of this publication may be reproduced, distributed or transmitted in any form or by any means, without prior written permission.

Tambeara Watkins /Freedom House Publishing
PO BOX 361631
Decatur Georgia 30036
www.freedomhouse-publishing.com

Zany Girl, natural hair questions / Tambeara Watkins . -- 1st ed.
ISBN 978-0-9983621-2-0

DEDICATION

I dedicate this Natural Hair book to all the beautiful young women in my life. Jessica, you have been natural for years now…let it go and embrace who you are. Hannah, you have no idea how beautiful the world of natural texture is for you. Quinny, you said "I want to go natural…but" just do it. Carly, you are so awesome for embracing your hair texture. Tamika, one word "Big Chop" and to Miss Reagan and Ava because of this book and the beautiful women in your life. You will grow up knowing exactly who you are and how to embrace it.
I love you all!

CONTENTS

	Acknowledgments	i
1	Am I Natural	Pg. # 6
2	Big Chop or Transition	Pg. # 8
3	Shampoo and Conditioner	Pg. # 19
4	Products	Pg. # 24
5	Night time care	Pg. # 31
6	Protective styles	Pg. # 33
7	Heat versus no heat	Pg. # 36
8	Exercise and swimming	Pg. # 42
9	Oils their Purpose	Pg. # 47
10	How to detangle	Pg. # 54
11	Coloring natural hair	Pg. #59
12	Foods to eat to promote growth	Pg. #65
13	Healthy hair growth tips	Pg. #84
14	Summer/ Winter Care	Pg. #73
15	Natural Hair Tools	Pg. #77

.Acknowledgments

Thank you to all those beautiful women that were brave enough to embrace your true self and pave the road for others to travel.

LET'S GO

Whenever I am out in public, I'm usually pinned on the grocery store aisle, in the clothing store with an armful of clothing to try on, or at the gas station pumping gas. It is always the same when I am asked how I styled my natural hair so cute. If they, themselves are naturals I get a series of questions (which I love to share) followed by I wish I knew what to do with my hair. If they have not fully committed to being natural yet then I get the following reasons as to why they are not ready. Please understand. I do not walk around showcasing my coils to solicit the next natural chic. I'm asked about my hair and when I say" just do it and learn in the process." Then, do I get the "I can't, I don't know, I wish, I will try, I can, I will and finally the" I just did it! Let's first understand where you are in the process. Read the following below and let's go from there.

I can't... is a quitter

I love your hair , but I could never go natural, my hair will not do that or look like that. You must have good hair. Ah... really? We all have "good hair" you just need to embrace it and love it. I tell you what, after my big chop I began to look at all the natural beauties online and could not wait to reach that point in my hair journey. I embrace each phrase or length moment by moment. Time seemed to fly by and before long years had passed me by and I was now the beauty that everyone admired. Not because of the length , but because I love my hair and who I am with it. I have confidence and own who I am and that is what attracts people to you.

I don't know... is too lazy

There is never a reason to say " I do not know." We live in an information overload world and anything you want to know is available to you, unless you are just sheer lazy and don't want to go after it. Making excuses as to why you don't know something is also laziness. We all have to deal with this part of learning about this new texture of hair coming from our head. It can be overwhelming if you let it or it can be very easy, it depends on your lifestyle and how you receive the information. Some people can take on loads of information and be ok with that, while others can only take on style by style information to make it easier. Either way let's take on an attitude to learn and grow healthy hair.

I wish I could... is a dreamer

Oh… I wish I could just go natural, but…whatever reason they have to give. It's ok to be a wisher. You just have not reached the level of confidence to move forward. Keep learning and before long you will just do it!

I might... is waking up

The one that says "I might" has the information and just waiting for the "right time." Guess what the time will never be right except right now. You are sitting on a fence trying to make the perfect decision at the perfect time. The whole point of being natural is to acquire freedom and liberation. So, let it go and make a decision. Either way you decide there will be people waiting to embrace you and your choice. So don't feel bad if you are not ready to become a natural girl. It just means you are not ready.

I will try... is on her feet

This person is learning to embrace, but unsure of the outcome and has to give herself a way out, thinking " if this is too much work, I will go back to a relaxer." She tells herself this to reassure herself that you are not making a wrong decision, just trying something different. The problem with this is that you have not clearly made a decision to fully commit no matter what. It's ok… you just need to get the revelation of why you are doing this. Believe me it's not for fun, even though we make it look that way. It can be mentally challenging in the beginning; that is why you have to become committed to staying in the ring until the battle is won!

I can... is on her way

The "I can" person is learning to walk into this new phase unsure, careful, but her feet still moves with lots of guidance. She has to connect with someone else that has her texture, whether

it be blogs, books, or a live person. She seeks out people wherever she goes to gain confidence and ask questions. She feels more confidence in the presence of other naturals. It empowers her, but when she is alone she has to connect to her usual source of encouragement. She still wears weave and wigs, not for pleasure or to change her look, but because she is still learning the confidence walk. Keep going you are almost there!

I will... is at work

This person has been in the "I can" long enough and now has the confidence and resources to pull this off. She asserts herself and ready to defend her territory from naysayers. She has learned to brush off negative comments and keep moving. She is committed and excited about her journey.

I did... is now in control

Congratulations! You have made a beautiful decision to embrace the hair that you were born with. This person is the trendsetter for her co-workers, friends, and family. Everyone can't wait until she arrives just to see how she will have her hair styled. She has been on this journey long enough that she now wants her body to match what she is accomplishing with her hair. She may dab in natural or organic foods, adopt a regular exercise regimen, and even rid her life of anything that does not bring her peace. She wants to be in harmony with the earth. If it rains , so what she has the perfect up-do hair style that would sustain in the rain, if it's humid out , no problem whatever is going on outside there is no frustration with her hair because she knows that she can easily turn one hairstyle into another style with a little eco styler or flaxseed gel, water, bobbin pins, or a ponytail holder. She stays equipped and ready to take on whatever the hair day brings.

Chapter 1
AM I NATURAL?

Dear Zany Girl,

I have been natural for two years, but I get my hair straighten every two weeks. I'm not comfortable wearing my natural curl pattern or a frizzy fro. I had a discussion with my friend who is also natural and very much comfortable sporting her twist out, wash n go, and fro at times. She stated that I was not considered natural because I get my hair straighten with heat. Please explain what natural hair really is about.

Dear Reader,

First let me say that defining your hair texture should be of less significance compared to healthy hair. The state that your hair is in should always matter first. This definition is not meant to stereotype people for choosing to continue with chemical hair straighteners or categorize those they have considered a natural lifestyle. We are all in different stages of our lives and the revelation of why we need to do certain things comes to us in many forms and at specific times, so show some love and embrace those that are not on your natural path.

Therefore, in an effort to define natural hair. I will give all definitions associated with natural hair for you to make an informed decision about the state of your hair.

The hair is considered natural when it is free from any and all chemicals that include relaxers, texturizers, colors, and any chemicals used to soften, slightly straighten, or relax the hair in any form.

Some people have colored and experienced a slightly loose alter in the curl pattern of the hair, therefore coloring can sometimes not be considered natural and sometimes others can color and experience no change. It really depends on your hair type. So just be mindful of what products you use to color your hair and if you would be ok with a slightly loose curl pattern.

Hair that has been straightened using a flat iron or blow dryer is still considered natural, because when products are washed from it; it will return to its natural state.

Your natural God-given curly, coily , or wavy hair in its natural state or heat straighten is beautiful and deserves to be embraced no matter where you are in your healthy hair journey.

CHAPTER 2
BIG CHOP OR TRANSITION

Dear Zany Girl,

I'm considering going all natural however, I'm not sure if I should do the big chop or transition into my new look. I want to keep my length because I'm not sure how I will look with short natural hair. What do you suggest and did you "big chop or transition?"

Dear Reader,

I encourage you to do whatever is comfortable for you- don't push it or rush the process. If the big chop is ultimately your goal, then I would suggest that you transition for a few months, then big chop when you have enough new growth that you are comfortable wearing. If your goal is never to big chop then definitely learn about caring for your hair while transitioning. I must say that you will be uncomfortable at first, but when you get all the compliments and attention from other natural women you will love it! You should enjoy the different stages of being natural. The most important part is the journey of being naturally free not the destination of long hair.

I transitioned for four months before I big chopped. It was the best decision ever. There is such an overwhelming feeling of liberation that comes with the "big chop" it cannot be explained verbally or in text format.

You just feel free.

Big Chop

What is the big chop?
By definition it is the process of cutting the relaxed ends of your hair off and leaving only the unprocessed texture.

Should I big chop myself or go to a salon?
Do whatever you feel comfortable doing. Although, you may want to visit a salon or barber shop to get rid of the relaxed ends. Many people have big chopped themselves at home and then went to a salon or barber to complete the look. It's all about comfort and finding someone that you trust.

How do I face criticism about my decision?
The longer you are natural the more your confidence will expand. It's not uncommon that you may feel a little uncomfortable with your new texture, however do not let the negative or ignorant comments of others to dictate your decision. Take the criticism, filter it , keep what you need to push forward and trash the rest.

I work, school, kids, etc.… will I have the time to give my hair the attention that it needs?
It may be best to find protective styles where you don't have to care for your hair for days or even a week. Do style your hair for your lifestyle and when you have free time you can do more relaxed

styles like a twist out and wash and go styles. These styles will need some form of night time care to have good results the next day.

How do I accept my texture?

You just accept it! It's yours to own, no matter what it looks like. Do not get caught up in another's texture by comparison or wishing you had a certain type of curls or coils. All textures are beautiful and should be celebrated as is.

How important is it to be patient during the process after I big chop?

You should be in no rush to reach a certain destination. Enjoy where you are in your hair growth. It will grow. So focus on making sure that it grows healthy. When you view styles online, be sure to stay with others that's in your length group, so that you do not get impatient with looking at another's length. It's ok to view others lengths as long as you are doing it for inspiration and not a comparison.

Here are a few things to consider before the big chop

Is the big chop for me ?

The big chop is not the only way to reach natural hair, however it's the quickest and easiest way to reach your goals.

Am I willing to accept my texture no matter what ?

While you look at the most beautiful natural coils or curls flowing and bouncing on the head of another. You visualize the same on your own head…wrong. Please allow your texture to come through and embrace it with fullness. Many women get into this misconception of textures. Yours is yours and hers is hers.

Can I experiment with products?

You will have to experiment with different products at different stages in your growth until you find what works for you. Keep in mind everything does not work for everyone.

Will I let the negativity affect my confidence?

There will always be naysayers in our lives no matter what we attempt to accomplish. Cutting your hair off to grow natural hair will be no different. I received negativity from friends and family in the beginning of my big chop. However when they saw the rapid and healthy growth of my hair and how I stood my ground of confidence and rocked my hair styles they began to ask how can they too can go natural.

Am I willing to do the work?

Learning about your new texture is work and natural hair does not give you the excuse to be lackadaisical in your hair regimen and not care for your hair. You have to be willing to put forth the effort to get the results.

Pros of big chop

1. You will only have one texture to deal with versus two texture if you are transitioning. Most people find it easier to adjust quicker with the one texture.

2. The maintenance of a big chop is awesome. It becomes fascinating to watch your hair grow and to do length checks to record your growth.

3. Water becomes your friend instead of your enemy. Swimming, exercising, and even the rain leaves you with a no hair fright attitude.

Cons of big chop

1. You could find that you do not like how you look with short hair. When this happens people will resort to weaves and wigs until they reach a comfortable length.

2. You will have to deal with the opinions of others, but who cares they will get over it and pretty soon asking you questions on how they too can achieve the look. People generally want to see if you will stick with it and when you do they will back off. Remember your change/ growth will make your friends or family uncomfortable.

3. There are very limited styling options with a big chop, but isn't that the point. You will want to just enjoy your new freedom of less maintenance and more control.

Transitioning

What is transitioning?

First, it's more about transitioning your mindset to become this "all natural woman" then it's about not wanting to chop off all of your hair and look like a cute boy. Many have said " I don't want to look like a boy" but let me tell you what a great feeling it was for me; to be free and free and free. However , if transiting is your choice then embrace it with much love. Transitioning is retaining both new natural texture and your old relaxed ends while trimming gradually to rid your hair of the relaxed ends and retaining length at the same time. You will never have to experience the big chop if you continue with this path until you reach a comfortable length.

Should I straighten/press my hair during the transition?

Okay… out with the old and in with the new texture that is. Why would you want your new and fabulous texture to match your old relaxed hair. Of course, you will be tempted to pressed, but please consider enjoying your coils, curls, and kinks. If you decide to press your hair to be sure you are well informed and/or make sure the stylist is as well to avoid heat damage. Just remember anything done too often is not good at all and the health of your hair is what is important.

Can I use texturizers ?
This is maybe a very common question amongst naturals. So, let's clear this up by saying that texturizers and relaxers have pretty much the same chemicals. The difference is the amount of time that you would leave it on your hair. It is still a chemical and if your goal is to be chemical free, then well, I think you know the rest. So, stay the course and learn your new texture instead of trying to adjust it.

What should I avoid while transitioning?
Naysayers! It is easy for people who are not in your shoes or position to be opinioned about your life's journey. Surround yourself with positive , but honest people. Remember people don't generally like change and when you began to change; it will make them uncomfortable and they will want to pull you back into their comfort zone.

What styles should I wear while transitioning?
You will want to wear styles that blend your two textures together with ease like; flat twists with a roller at the end to curl it, take down dried cornrows for a great style, various roller sets or an updo with a bun. (see section on protective styles) Protective styles are a great addition to these as well. Let's not forget about our favorite wigs or sewn in weaves to give us great styles as well while transitioning.

Can I use my old products while transitioning?

You may find that the products you used in the past may not necessary work best for your new texture. You will want to consider more natural friendly products that do not contain heavy oils or grease. Just remember that natural hair works better with water based products. You can buy products or have fun and make them yourself. Don't be too hard on yourself if you get overwhelmed with all the products. Just know what you are doing to your hair and find that product that fits your needs.

How to avoid breakage during transitioning?

Not getting enough moisture to your hair could be a huge problem while transitioning. You are dealing with two textures and it will require you moisture daily or deep condition weekly. Know your hair, if you have oily hair, then of course, you will not need to moisture too often, however most natural hair is dry and will require lots of moisture. Understand the weakest and strongest part of your hair is called the line of demarcation, where the breakage will mostly likely occur if the hair is not treated properly. Where previously processed hair meets unprocessed hair. Keeping a spray bottle with half water and half oil of your choice is a great mist/moisturizer for your hair at night before bed or anytime you need to add moisture. It is also equally important to trim every six to twelve weeks for healthy hair.

Dealing with two different textures

The frustrating part of transiting is dealing with two textures. You now need to find hairstyles that will work best for the two textures. Choosing the right styles are important in maintaining control. You will want to make sure you are styling with protective styles and styles like twists, braid out that will blend your two different textures and hide those straight ends until you are ready to chop them off completely.

Chapter 3
SHAMPOO AND CONDITIONER

Dear Zany Girl,

Please help! There are so many shampoos and conditioners out there. I'm not sure which I should use for my hair. I hear people say don't use products that have this or that in it. To be honest I'm just overwhelmed and in need of a shampoo that will work for me .

Dear Reader,

I totally understand your concern. When I began my journey I tried several shampoos and conditioners. Some made my hair feel worse, while others left my hair feeling great. I believe the only true way to determine what works for your hair is to try it. Look for samples at the beauty supply stores, hair shows, etc… there are even some hair salons that will give you samples because they sell the products in the salon. I volunteered at a natural hair event and received enough samples and retail size products that lasted me for months. I was able to try it out on small sections of my hair and then purchase the larger containers, if I liked them.

How do I know if I need a clarifying shampoo?//
Know your hair. If you see any signs of products build up or white residue on the hair that don't wash off so easily. Maybe you are a heavy product user, then you may need to use a clarifying shampoo monthly to rid your hair of product build up that a regular shampoo will not do. You will notice that your natural curls will pop back to life once all clean and respond to your normal products again. Not really into clarifying shampoos? Well an alternative would be bentonite clay, apple cider vinegar, or baking soda added to your regular shampoo.

How often should I shampoo?

Different textures, products, climates, and lifestyles will determine how often you will need to shampoo your hair. Follow your own hair regimen that fits your lifestyle. Attempt to limit your shampoos to as less an often and replace with a co-wash to avoid dryness. Some ladies can shampoo as often as every week , while others can hold out monthly. It would be a great idea to co-wash with a cleansing conditioner in between washes to help retain moisture into the hair. Shampooing too often can result in dryness and breakage of the hair. You will need to evaluate your hair for product build-up and dirt to decide if a shampoo is needed over a co-wash. Just remember that retaining moisture on clean hair is important and needs to be taken seriously for healthy hair.

What is co-washing and why should I do it?

Co-washing is basically "conditioner washing". You are cleaning your hair with a conditioner or labeled in store as co-wash. This method will help to retain/add moisture to your hair oppose to a regular shampoo that will take the moisture out, then you will have to put it back by using a conditioner. Many people find this popular co-washing method great for their in between hair shampoos. You can co-wash as often as you need to. Again, always evaluate your hair before doing anything to it to find out what it needs.

How to choose a shampoo for my hair?

Shampoo tends to be harsh on African American hair because of "dryness" that seems to be a problem for us, therefore it's important to find a shampoo that retains moisture instead of shampoos that strip the moisture from your hair. There are certain things that you need to look for when selecting a shampoo. First, find a shampoo that will be gentle enough not to strip your hair of its natural oils by avoiding alcohol in shampoos. Next, you want to find a shampoo that will maintain your normal pH-Balance of around 5 for your hair. You will want to look for a shampoo with a pH-Balance of between 4.5- 5.5. Last , you need a shampoo with some natural oils like, avocado, coconut oil, olive oil and so forth. Be sure to look for a hydrating shampoo that is creamier as to not dry out your hair(also see the chapter on products).

Tips for shampooing hair
- ❖ Always detangle hair before washing to prevent matting
- ❖ Wash hair in sections for longer hair by using clips, ponytail holders
- ❖ Use shampoos that are sulfate free
- ❖ Consider adding oils or conditioner to hair before washing to retain moisture during washing.
- ❖ Hair is fragile when wet, therefore be gentle when combing or brushing to prevent breakage.
- ❖ Always condition afterward to put back moisture

deep conditioners

Dry or brittle hair? Breakage or hair splitting? It may be time to deep conditioner to fortify the hair with moisture. Deep conditioners can be disguised as deep, masque, restorative, strengthens, or treatment. They will enter into the hair follicle and make deposits into the hair strand to repair any damage. Most people saturate the hair with the creamy conditioners , then cover with plastic cap and sit under a dryer for about 20 minutes or why not, just sleep with it in our hair overnight, then rinse with cool water to close the pore and retain the moisture. You can deep conditioner every two weeks or once a month depending on your hair needs. (also see chapter on products).

Tips for deep conditioner

- ❖ Use heat under a hooded dryer to expand your hair shaft so that the conditioner can penetrate the hair.
- ❖ Cool water rinse to close the cuticle to retain nutrients

Protein Conditioners

Protein conditioners are a good way to restore moisture that will help with elasticity, so that breakage is not a problem. Hair is made of protein, therefore you are reinforcing its strength when you add to it. You can feel free to add natural oils that penetrate the hair shaft like coconut oil and olive oil for extra moisture. You can use protein treatments as often as once a month. Protein treatments can be used as a preventive method to keep dry and brittle hair at bay or as a routine to healthy hair.

Tips for the protein conditioner
- ❖ Water should always be the first ingredient in any products
- ❖ Keep balance- do not over moisture (soft and mushy) or under saturating (dry and brittle).
- ❖ The product should say "protein".
- ❖ If you experience breaking and shedding, it may be in indication that a protein conditioner is needed.

CHAPTER 4
PRODUCTS

Dear Zany Girl,
There are so many products for natural hair that I get overwhelmed when choosing and end up buying too many products. I have often been called a "product junkie". How can I be sure what works to cut down on the amount of products that I have to buy.

Dear Reader,
There are many products out there that do different things with your hair, so get informed about what each product does and how it works for you to get the results. Sometimes when we are not sure how to use a product we can take a negative attitude about it and tell others that "it does not work". When really, we are just not sure how to use it. The best advice when selecting products are; get product reviews from others and watch videos on how others may be using and mixing with other products to get the best results.

Twist defining cream
 If you want defined twist out styles, then this product is for you. It will give you a smooth and moisturized look and feel. You can add the twist defining cream to soaking wet hair for a tighter curl pattern or on damp stretched hair for an elongated looser curl pattern.

- ❖ Shiny well defined twist out styles
- ❖ Hydrates hair
- ❖ Helps to prevent shedding and thinning of the hair
- ❖ Produces strong, lasting definition
- ❖ Air drying is recommended, but feel free to use a hooded dryer as needed
- ❖ Always use a wide tooth comb

curling jelly
You will want to finger rake or wide tooth comb this product in your hair for a great wash n go. It will define your coils and curls when used while hair is soaking wet. You can air dry or set hair under a hooded dryer . Be careful not to us too much product, as it will become sticky and clumpy droplets on the hair, which will result in flaking.

- ❖ Defines coils and curls
- ❖ Reduces frizz

- ❖ Reduces shrinkage and enhances stretched hair
- ❖ Seals in moisture
- ❖ Curl booster
- ❖ After application, DO NOT DISTURB the hair until it is completely dry (it will cause the hair to frizz)

Double Butter Cream

If you are looking for a soft twist out , then grab this product. Apply a little or a lot depending on your hair's need for moisture. Feel free to use with twist defining cream for a deeper set of style and remember do not overuse a sit cause a dull appearance.

- ❖ Seals in moisture
- ❖ Softness and shine
- ❖ Repairs split end and strengthen hair

Hydration Elation

This moistening product will hydrate your thirsty strands and enhance manageability and overall health of your hair. Treat your hair to a Hydration Elation treatment every two to three weeks to establish a good habit of hydrating your hair.

- ❖
  - ❖ Shine
  - ❖ Deep moisturizer
  - ❖ Smooth cuticle layer
  - ❖ Stimulate the scalp and hair roots
  - ❖ Treat every 2-3 weeks

Smoothing Gel
Use this smoothing gel to smooth down any style that requires a secure hold and shine. Just keep in mind the less oil on your hair, the more of a hold you will have.
- ❖ Adds shine
- ❖ Secure hold
- ❖ Moisturizes
- ❖ Won't dry out, harden the hair

Hair Milk
When you are in need of moisture and manageability hair milk will be your friend. It is light enough not to weight your hair down and will give it the shine it needs. Overuse may cause hair to appear dull in appearance.
- ❖ Shines
- ❖ Hydrates
- ❖ softens

Clarifying shampoo
This shampoo will remove product build up and impurities from the hair and the scalp. The clarifying shampoo of choice should be gentle enough to cleanse without stripping the hair. Remember to condition before and after every shampoo to restore and or retain moisture.
- ❖ Use when build up is needed to be removed

- ❖ It should prevent hair from drying out
- ❖ It should leave hair moisturized
- ❖ It should not be too harsh that it strips the hair of its natural oils.

Co-wash Cleanse

You can co-wash with this cleanser often as daily. It will not strip the hair of needed moisture and works great for in between shampoo days.

- ❖ Gentle cleanse
- ❖ Maintains moisture
- ❖ Detangle
- ❖ Promotes healthy hair growth

Cleansing Puddings

This is another option to cleanse your hair in between shampoo washes. It will not strip natural oils from your hair. It will leave your hair clean from environmental impurities and shed scalp debris

- ❖ Cleanses hair of residue and product build-up
- ❖ Moisturizes
- ❖ Soothing scalp treatment
- ❖ Promotes a healthy environment hair growth

Curl Revitalizer sprays

Get rid of that day-old- look, use a curl revitalizer to bring hair back to life. This lightweight spray will not weight down your coils or curls. It will leave your hair soft and frizz free.

- ❖ Control frizz
- ❖ Soften hair
- ❖ Revitalizes curls and coils
- ❖ Lightweight mist

Spray Moisturizer

Feel free to use this product with twist defining cream for added moisture and shine. If you are looking for something to protect your hair during hot summer months and cold winter days then, spray the moisture in your in your and rub gently on hair.

- ❖ moisturizes the scalp
- ❖ soften and shine
- ❖ seals in moisture
- ❖ protects against weather damage

Detangling Conditioner

The detangling conditioner is a great way to release your tangles. Apply to soaking wet hair, detangle, then you can use it as a leave it. If you apply too much then , it's ok just do a light rinse to remove some of the product and styles as usual.

- ❖ Provides easier release of tangle
- ❖ Can use as a leave in after detangling
- ❖ Moisturizes and shine

- ❖ Strengthen hair and repair damage
- ❖ Hydrate and nourish hair

Hair soap

Hair soap, otherwise known as shampoo bars are a great natural alternative to shampoo. They are created specifically for natural textured hair They have a huge advantage over shampoo because of the soap bar later less , thus stripping the hair of needed moisture. These are amazing because they can also be used for hair and entire body. There are a variety of bars that contains carrot seed oil, shea butter, honey, yogurt, and so forth. So, enjoy these shampoo bars , protect your hair while toning your scalp.

- ❖ Rich ,cleansing moisturizing bar
- ❖ Hydrates hair
- ❖ Soft hair
- ❖ Protects against heat and chemical damage
- ❖ shine

Leave in conditioner

Leave in conditioners that leave our hair feeling soft and manageable when applied to clean, detangled hair. This product should leave your hair with added moisture and shine. It easily prepares your hair for styling with ease.

- ❖ Strengthen hair
- ❖ Seals the cuticle layer
- ❖ Adds moisture and shine
- ❖ Eases wet combing

Chapter 5
NIGHT TIME CARE

Dear Zany Girl,

I really need some advice on maintaining my styles during the night. I'm usually too tired to do anything to my hair at night and just fall asleep after a long day. The next morning my style is ruined and I result in my bun or pin and tuck style as I run out the door for work.

Dear Reader,

A night time care is important to preserving your styles and protecting your hair from breakage. A satin pillow case if you allow your hair to be free or a satin bonnet to cover your hair takes little to no effort in preserving certain styles. Preparation is essential to your night time care. Keep items near the bed or within reach bedtime. There are different quick and easy methods that are available to help with night time care. I have listed a few below to assist you. Hope it helps.

Why do I need nighttime care?
Night time care is essential for your natural hair. It aids in the health of your hair. You will retain moisture, prevent unwanted breakage, and preserve your hairstyles for the next day.

Methods- Bunning and Pineapple
You should not have to re-do your styles nightly. An easier way to preserve such styles would be to use the " pineapple method" by pulling all hair to the top of the head and securing with a ponytail holder. Careful to preserve the curls at the top. In the morning just add oil and shake or manipulate to get your style back.

Another method will be the "Bunning method" which is similar to the pineapple by piling hair on the head and pinning the longer length hair on the head into a bun.

It is important to develop a night time routine to protect your style and hair. You will appreciate it in the morning when you do not have to wake up to a matted mess or have to restyle your hair every morning. So, decide what is right for you and keep it simple.

Oh , yeah…do does not forget to add your night time oils.

Chapter 6
PROTECTIVE STYLES

Dear Zany Girl,
Are protective styles necessary for natural hair? Should I include them in my hair routine? I have noticed a lot of natural that wear protective

Dear Reader,
Protective styles are great! But are they for you? They are a fun and versatile way to add different styles to your hair. The great part is that you can wear them for a night out or a week long. They are awesome for workouts and great for retaining length because there is no combing involved. You can choose to wear them or not.

Can your hair retain length without protective styles?

Yes! Protective styles can be used for some as a form of length retention, however it is not necessary for length retention for those that have hair that grows no matter what you do to it. It does help, however to retain length because you are not combing your hair and causing breakage.

Is your hair prone to locs?

If so, then, you should limit the number of days that you wear your styles. Know your texture and what your hair will do. For some, if you keep twist out in too long it can lock your locs together.

Is there an alternative to protective styling

Yes, low manipulation styling can be used as an alternative to protective styling to retain length. You will want to work styles that allow you to go into a second hairstyle like a twist out can be used as an up do the next day or so. Recycling hair styles are great for retaining length along with finger detangling over comb detangling.

Are protective styles for you

Just because you are natural does not mean that protective styling is right for you. It is known that protective styles are a great way to retain length and to show off a new style, however it may not be the best thing to do for all. Here are a few hints that protective styling is not for you .

Protective styles for transitioning

Protective styling is great for transitioning natural. It allows you blend both textures together into a wonderful style. Such styles like Flat twists, cornrows, wet sets, twist out, and braid outs

Tips for protective styles
- ❖ If you have scalp condition, protective styles are not for you
- ❖ You should value the health of your hair over length retention
- ❖ Regular deep treatments should be included in your styling
- ❖ Decrease your combing for length retention
- ❖ Decide if protective styling is right for you.

CHAPTER 7
HEAT VERSUS NO HEAT

Dear Zany Girl,
I often dry my hair by various method of a blow dryer or hooded dryer for my desired styles. I have noticed some that there is some strand of my hair that will not revert back to its natural coiled state. Please help!

Dear Reader,
If you choose to use heat , then you should definitely use precaution and protect your hair strands against the heat that you apply to it. Heat damage is real and can cause your coils, kinky, curls not to revert back to its natural state, leaving you frustrated with stringy strands. So, let's talk heat protection.

HEAT

Why do I need a heat protectant
Direct heat is damaging to your hair shaft and needs to be protected.; using a heat protectant will prevent the full transference of heat to your hair. It will aid in reducing any type of damages to the hair. Your next step is to find a heat protectant that you like.

How to choose a heat protectant
Like choosing any product, you need to select a protectant that works well with your hair and trying different products may be the answer. Sometimes you know with the first product and sometimes you try out several products before you find what you like.

Tips for choosing a heat protectant
- serums and oils will work better than water-based products
- look for healthy ingredients to aid in the health of your hair
- look for ingredients like; silicones and polymers
- natural ingredients like; grape seed oil, sunflower, olive, and coconut oil

Drying/ Styling natural Hair with heat

Some women cringe at the thought of putting heat on their hair, while others delight in a stretched out wash n go. It's your hair and your choice whether to use heat or not. There are various methods of drying your natural hair. You need to know the importance of how to dry your hair. For those that use the heat method. Not knowing can result in heat damage and that would be a shame after all of the hard work you put into growing healthy hair. So, let's get informed and change or create new and healthy habits of taking care of our hair when using heat.

Tips to drying your hair
- after shampoo towel dry with a microfiber towel to absorb the majority of the water. (do not blow dry soaking wet hair)
- put hair in sections using twists, braids or clips to make it easier to apply the conditioner
- apply your leave in conditioner
- apply an oil that seals in the moisture(see oils for hair chapter)
- keep the twists, cornrows, braids, or whatever your method until the hair air dries and ready for styling.

Blow Drying

Blow drying should not be a part of your normal routine, but sometimes it happens. If you plan to wear a flat iron hairstyle , then you may want to include a blow dryer in your style option. Now, the important part is that you protect your hair against the heat from the blow dryer by ensuring that you have one of many kinds of dryers like a thermal ionic technology blow dryer along with a heat protection.

Tips for blow drying

- ❖ Towel dry first, do not blow dry soaking wet hair
- ❖ Always use a heat protectant to protect against heat damage
- ❖ Ionic technology blow dryer or similar technology
- ❖ Use wide tooth comb to minimize breakage, avoid small tooth comb

Hooded Dryer

You may want to use the hooded dryer for setting twists or braid styles that may normally take forever to dry on thicker hair. Try to let it dry half way and then air dry the rest so that the hair will not be too dried out from the heat. Use the hooded dryer for deep conditioners or hair mask. Remember you will still need to use a heat protectant on your hair of you plan on sitting under the dryer for a long period of time.

Drying/ Styling with NO HEAT

Of course , there are ways to achieve dried or stretched hair without heat. You may not be a fan of heat for your hair and that is ok. Just opt for air drying your styles and use methods of stretching the hair without heat.

- ❖ Banning method requires that you section hair using ponytail holders and then began wrapping several ponytail holders along the length of the hair until you reach the ends. Let air dry and then remove for a stretched style
- ❖ Braids or twists are done in larger sections, then secure to head with bobby pins by slightly pulling on the hair in a wrapping motion, allow to air dry then take hair down and enjoy stretched hair with a slight wave in texture

Air Drying

Air drying will be your best friend to drying natural hair. Yes, it may take a lot longer for your hair to dry, which is why you will have to plan your air drying hairstyles ahead of time.

Chapter 8
EXERCISE AND SWIMMING

Dear Zany Girl,

There are two things that I enjoy the most; swimming and exercising. How can I protect or prepare my natural hair for either? Also, how can I preserve my twist out during a workout?

Dear Reader,

Swimming is such a fun and relaxing way to enjoy the summer. You should not have to worry about what your hair is doing or how much chlorinated water is being soaked in by your hair. However, contact with chlorine can take a toll on your hair and need to be protected to survive the summer months Exercise, however will need a different approach to protecting your hair against your own sweat during a workout and preserving your hairstyle

.

How to prevent chlorine damage

Enjoy the sun and swim as often as you like, just be sure to protect your hair by doing a few things, because chlorine is a chemical disinfectant added into water to kill bacteria, oils, and dirt and your scalp produce oil to protect your scalp. The chlorine strips your hair of its natural oils, thus making it really dry and causing damage. You will need to wet the hair with tap water first, this will allow your hair to be filled up with as much tap water as possible to prevent the hair soaking in chlorine water. Be sure to shampoo afterward with a shampoo that will lift the chlorine from your hair. If you swim every day then you will need to shampoo and condition every day. If all possible try to use a swim cap to protect your hair and remember that chlorine does not rinse out with water alone.

Tips to prevent chlorine damaged hair
- ❖ Saturate your hair with water
- ❖ Use a swim cap
- ❖ Rinse after swimming
- ❖ Always shampoo after swimming
- ❖ Moisturize after shampoo

How to repair chlorine damaged hair

If you find that you have enjoyed the water a little too much and have not paid very much attention to protecting your hair, then you need to evaluate your tresses to see if there may have been chlorine damage. If so, follow the tips blow to repair damage You will know because your hair will feel really dry, frizzy on the ends and it will matt up easily.

Tips to repair chlorine damaged hair

- ❖ Clarifying shampoo or add baking soda to your regular shampoo
- ❖ Apple cider vinegar rinse will remove the chlorine buildup
- ❖ If your scalp is really dry, then use products to replenish moisture
- ❖ Coconut oil will repair damaged hair caused by chlorine
- ❖ Protein treatments will replenish the protein that has been stripped from your hair
- ❖ Deep conditioners should be done by weekly to restore moisture
- ❖ You can always seek professional help and see if you need to cut the damaged ends or just repair.

Exercise

Exercise is not just a task, but a lifestyle for most. If you exercised longer than you have been natural, then you will be puzzled on what to do wityour natural tresses. Many do not have the time to rinse, shampoo, or co-wash their hair after every workout. Most time you are going from gym to work or gym to an event. Even though most gyms have showers that you can freely wash your hair after a workout, you may not want to because daily washing will produce a dry and itchy scalp. . Remember that all hair and people are different. So, anytime you adopt any regimen you should always keep it specific to your needs and lifestyle. Most people sweat from their scalp, while others sweat a lot less from their scalp, therefore you will need to pay attention to how your hair react to a workout There are a few things that you can do to protect your hair during a workout.

Styling your hair after a workout

Now, that your workout is complete and you have your hair in a pineapple or ponytail, what now? You will want to dry your roots while in an updo and gently take your hair while concentrating on the drying the roots. Your twist out or braid out should be just fine. On the other hand, the sweat doesn't bother my hair at all. Air dry is all I usually need.

Tips to protect your hair during a workout
- ❖ Use ponytail holders and buns to protect during workout
- ❖ Use protective styles during workout days

Chapter 9
OILS AND THEIR PURPOSE

Dear Zany Girl,
Can you help me find the best oils for my hair? There are so many oils out there in "natural oil/ butter world" that I can get a bit overwhelmed by what to use or when I should use it. Please help with the best selection of oils/ butter to use.

Dear Reader,
While all oils/butter are good for your natural hair, however you do need to know what oils do what for your hair and how to use them in combinations with other hair products. There is a selection of oils and butter that you may want to keep on hand at all time to use simultaneously.

Shea Butter
- Acts as a layer to seal in moisture on the hair strand
- Reduces moisture from being lost
- Dry or sensitive skin
- Anti-aging- anti-wrinkling
- Protects hair and skin from the sun
- Prevents dryness of the hair and skin

Aloe Butter
- Light and melts to touch
- Moisturizer
- Mixture of aloe vera and coconut oil

Cupuacu Butter
- Soften and smooth the hair
- Retains moisture
- Can add to your conditioner

Coconut Oil
- Another perfect for sealing oil in the hair.
- Will add shine and strength to hair.
- Popular for natural hair
- Leave in conditioner
- Will hydrate the hair
- Reduce the protein loss when used as a pre-wash / daily usage

Babassu Oil
- ❖ Similar to coconut oil
- ❖ Seals your ends
- ❖ Use as a pre-shampoo
- ❖ Non-greasy

Mineral Oil
- ❖ Frizz fighting
- ❖ Define your coils- it's known for forming curls by attracting the fibers together.
- ❖ Non-greasy
- ❖ Great for detangling curly hair
- ❖ Decrease damage from chemicals
- ❖ Works as a barrier to protect the hair

popular oils for the natural community. Coconut oil can be as a great leave-in conditioner.

Aloe Vera
- ❖ stops hair loss, can treat scalp issues,
- ❖ repair damage from heat
- ❖ Add into your shampoo or conditioner.
- ❖ For scalp conditions , just rub some on your scalp and rinse off. Leave on for about two hours
- ❖ This oil has an enzyme that stimulates hair follicles for growth..
- ❖ Use emphasize curls and waves
- ❖ Use to set wet hair with braids, roller set, twists out.

Glycerin
- Moisture retention
- Maybe better to use in combination with other oils or water
- Too much will become tacky and sticky on the hair
- Adds a kick to curls
- Reduce frizz and helps with the flexibility

Jojoba Oil
- acts as a moisture retainer over the hair strand.
- Nongreasy oil
- will give your hair a nice shine.
- Massage onto scalp to remove build up
- Helps dry and damaged hair
- Protects against damage from brushing and combing the hair

Olive Oil
- Great deep conditioner for hair
- Can penetrate the hair better than other oils
- Promotes scalp and prevent dandruff

Tea Tree Oil
- Soothes dry scalp
- Antiseptic, antibacterial and antifungal
- Dandruff
- Mix with sea salt for a facial scrub for acne
- Itchy scalp

Apricot Oil
- Easy absorption
- Shine
- Restore dry and damaged hair
- Rich in vitamin A and E

Kemp seed Oil
- Soften the scalp
- Great as a hair conditioner or
- Works well in preventing water loss
- Hair growth stimulator
- Strengthen the hair

Wheat germ Oil
- Hair treatment
- Aid in cell growth
- Easily absorbed
- Moisturizer
- Repair dry, damaged hair
- Restore shine

Sunflower Oil
- **Soften hair**
- **Add shine**
- **Prevents dryness and frizziness**
- **Can use as a conditioner**

Hazelnut Oil
- Light and easily absorbed
- Strengthen hair
- Apply before shampooing to preserve hair color

Soybean Oil
- Reduce moisture loss
- Scalp stimulator
- Moisture for dry hair
- Can use a deep conditioner

Sesame Oil
- Hair growth
- Have darkening qualities when massaged into hair
- Treat gray hair because of its darkening qualities
- Increases scalp circulation
- Regain hair health
- Natural sunscreen

Amla Oil
- Treatment for hair loss
- Prevent graying of hair
- Strengthen hair follicle
- Soothe dry , itchy scalp

Macadamia Oil
- Fight hair breakage
- Improves hair strength
- Elasticity
- Improve frizzy hair
- Hydrates dull hair

Rice Bran Oil
- Anti-aging
- Retain moisture
- Rejuvenate dull hair
- Add shine
- Protects against sun damage
- Fights dandruff
- Thicker hair and split ends

Grapeseed Oil
- Moisturizer and conditioner
- Reduces hair loss
- Strengthening of the hair
- Promotes hair growth
- Add shine
- Dry scalp

Safflower Oil
- Works as a sealant
- Use against humid weather
- Moisturizer

CHAPTER 10
HOW TO DETANGLE

Dear Zany Girl
I recently encountered the worst matted hair ever. I removed braids from my hair and then went right into washing it. Later , I found out that I should have followed some steps to detangling my hair before I wash. Please explain.

Dear Reader
Yes, believe it or not, but natural hair cannot just be washed in the same manner as when you had a relaxer. Natural hair tangles easier and you will need to take steps for the detangling weather you about washing or going into a second hairstyle. Detangling is very important for natural hair and doing it correctly will ensure you save much-needed length on your hair.

Why should I detangle

Detangling your hair is very important to retaining length. Is there a proper way to detangle? Oh sure! And many have learned the hard way. When you have a cute cut it's much simpler to run your fingers through your hair and detangle, however when you reach a length that requires you to section your hair before detangling, the process can be time-consuming and requires a little planning on your part. Here's why; improper planning can cost you length.

Detangle before a second hairstyle

We all know that one hairstyle can easily go into another style in between washes or co-washes. However, you may want to detangle certain styles before going into another style to keep down on hair matting or lessen your overall detangling time.

Detangle before washing

DO NOT TAKE DOWN BRAIDS, TWISTS OR SUCH STYLES AND DIVE RIGHT INTO A WASH! You will definitely have a tangled matted mess on your hands that could result in hours upon hours of detangling and loss of length. In extreme cases, it could lead to cutting off your tresses to rid the matted hair.

Dry Detangle

Dry detangling works best for hair that has major shrinkage when wet. It will be best to use the finger detangling method on dry hair, because a comb or brush may be too harsh on the hair.

Tips for dry detangling
- ❖ To get through this process it will be best to part the hair in sections
- ❖ work slowly to detangle using a conditioner that works best for your hair along with a mist of water.
- ❖ Careful not to saturate the hair and cause shrinkage.

Detangling matted and tangled hair

Detangling matted or badly detangled hair could be a worse nightmare for someone that has invested time in growing out her hair. The last thing we want to do is lose unintentional length in the process.

Tips for detangling matted hair
- ❖ Do not shampoo the hair or it will tangle or mat the hair even more
- ❖ Do not tear through hair, you will lose length if you do
- ❖ The conditioner soak method and a wide tooth comb may work best for this
- ❖ You may want to start at the root and comb to the end slowly and without forcing it straight through in one motion.
- ❖ Be patient

Finger detangling versus comb detangling

You will have to decide which method is best based on your hair and the given information that you know about comb and finger detangling. It is obvious that you will use both methods at different times and at different stages in your hair growth stages.

Tips to consider
- ❖ It can take hours to get through a detangling session
- ❖ Find a shorter method that works for you
- ❖ Keep detangling simple and enjoy your hair

Tips for Water and Oil Detangling
- ❖ Part hair in small sections to work from
- ❖ Only mist hair with oil and water when detangling
- ❖ You may comb the hair from the root to the end slowly to detangle

Tips for Conditioner Detangling
- ❖ Start on dry hair, do not wet hair for this method
- ❖ Add conditioner of your choice to hair. (finding one that has a good slip would be best for detangling)
- ❖ Heat can be applied to your conditioner ,

if needed.

Tips for Dry Detangling
- ❖ Do not shampoo the hair before detangling, this will cause unwanted shrinkage
- ❖ Finger detangling method will be more appropriate, since combs and brushes will be too harsh
- ❖ Washing the hair in sections after you have detangled would be best to preserve your detangled hair

Chapter 11
COLORING NATURAL HAIR

Dear Zany Girl,

I usually color my hair lighter in the summer in months and darker in the winter months when I relaxed my hair. I'm now all natural and want to protect my hair from the damage that I was doing to it previously. Is color safe for natural hair and how do I get the same color results?

Dear Reader,

Colors are beautiful and everyone wants or need a change once in a while. There are ways you can achieve your seasonal change without much harm to your natural hair. You will need to seek professional help if you are not comfortable with coloring. As always follow instructions given to you by the maker.

Hair Coloring Natural Hair

We all love the look of color on natural hair. Something about those colored kinky, coiled, curly tresses that gets you excited enough to try it! Is coloring your hair using chemicals good? No, but its healthier to color natural –unprocessed hair than it is to color chemically relaxed hair. You will also need to use precautions, preparations, and understand how to care for your colored hair.

Tips for natural hair
- ❖ Always do a strand test to ensure timing for best color results and to ensure you are not allergic to the product
- ❖ Do read the instructions, even if you have been coloring often when using a new product
- ❖ Deep condition after you color to restore moisture
- ❖ Seek professional help when you are unsure about the process

Oh... What I would give to undo the hair color mistakes

Just like anything else, you can make mistakes in hair coloring.

So, just be aware of what you want and if a mistake happens ; know that it can be fixed.

Tips on hair color mistakes

- ❖ Do not leave color on too long- use the allotted time indicated in the instructions, damage can occur
- ❖ The sink does not have enough pressure to wash out all of the chemicals from your hair, opt for the shower instead.
- ❖ If you have way too much hair, then get help with the process. You can have some missed areas and discolorations in certain areas.
- ❖ Just to be real; You may not get the color indicated on the box. Always have a back- up plan.
- ❖ Make sure you have more than enough product. Natural hair can be deceiving and may take more product than relaxed hair.

Examine the condition of your hair before coloring

Always take precaution before you color. If you have dry hair then do a moisture treatment that will get the moisture back before coloring. If you need a trim, then trim before coloring. Just make sure that your hair is at its healthiest state before putting in chemicals such as a color on your hair.

Don't ignore directions

Some of us love to do-it-yourself color at home. Something important to know, read the box instructions They are there for a reason. To walk you through the process for easily application. Even if you have been coloring for years, still look over the directions for minor changes or warning that may have been included.

Permanent Hair Color

Permanently coloring the natural hair means that the color will penetrate the hair cuticle, thus giving you a longer commitment to a color. Just keep in mind that permanent coloring will not "rinse out" like temporary colors, however it will fade over time with shampooing, therefore use sulfate free shampoo to help preserve your color.

Tips for permanent coloring
- ❖ Make sure hair is healthy
- ❖ You can add water to your home box color to lessen the strength
- ❖ Great coverage for gray hair

Temporary Hair Color

Yep, just that, temporary coloring or hair rinse. It will usually wash out within 6-8 shampoo washes. These will deposit color only and are not meant to lift your hair If you have a light hair color and want to temporarily darken it, then a rinse will be a better fit for your hair

Tips for Temporary coloring
- ❖ Wear gloves when washing hair, color will run on hands and towels when drying
- ❖ No ammonia and no peroxide in these products, therefore safe to use without the use of chemicals
- ❖ Temporary colors will stain your gray hair and not wash away completely

Semi- Permanent Hair Color

This one has a more lasting effect on the hair. It may contain a small amount of peroxide only to deepen the color, not enough to lift the hair. It will definitely last a lot longer than a temporary color.

Tips for Semi-Permanent coloring
- ❖ Usually lasts 6-8 weeks
- ❖ Oils will cause the color to come off on hands.

Highlights

Highlighting your hair can be a good contrast to your existing color. It can add dimension or depth to any area of your hair or the whole head.

Tips for highlighting your natural hair
- ❖ Try a tint over a bleach
- ❖ You can color using small sections or larger ones
- ❖ Seek professional help as needed

Henna

Henna is a wonderful way to color your hair without the usage of chemicals. Henna is plant based and will not cause side effects. It has benefits that will not only color your hair , but strengthen and shine.

Tips for Henna
- ❖ Will cover grays
- ❖ Will give highlights to grays if rest of hair is dark
- ❖ Mix the henna according to the directions listed
- ❖ You can purchase henna already premixed or you can purchase the powder and mix yourself
- ❖ Henna comes in a variety of beautiful colors

CHAPTER 12
FOODS TO PROMOTE GROWTH

Dear Zany Girl,
Deciding to be natural with my hair has encouraged me to think about the foods that I put inside my body. While I have adopted a healthier lifestyle I would like to know what foods are good for my hair so that I can make sure have them in my diet

Dear Reader,
Everything that we do to our body is important to our health and the health of our hair. We want to maximize as much growth as we can in whatever way that we can so I have listed some foods that are beneficial to the growth and well- being of our hair.

Foods to eat to promote growth

You may ask, are there really foods that you can eat to promote hair growth? The answer is... yes! While genetics play a major role in how our hair grows, eating the right foods with the nutrients that your hair needs will maximize your growth. There are certain dietary needs that should be included in your diet for hair growth and overall heath.

Protein

Getting enough protein will ensure the best possible growth since hair is made up mostly of protein.

- Eggs
- Soy
- Fish and seafood
- Poultry
- Nuts
- Greek yogurt

Omega 3

Healthy fats are really good for hair growth , nail and skin.

- Avocado
- Walnuts
- Flax seeds
- Salmon
- Pumpkin seeds

Vitamin C
Vitamin C is great for fighting dandruff, prevent split ends, stops hair loss, thicker hair ,and even prevents graying of the hair.

- sweet potatoes
- tomatoes
- strawberries
- papaya
- kiwi

Zinc
Zinc helps to produce natural oil for your scalp that works to give you healthy hair, moisturize hair, and a conditioned scalp. It helps to minimizing hair loss.
- Oysters
- Beef
- shrimps
- Eggs
- nuts

Antioxidant beta carotene
Antioxidant beta-carotene provides consistent hair growth, fights dandruff, and glowing hair.
- Spinach
- Mangoes
- Apricots
- Cantaloupe
- Carrots

Iron

Iron is important because it helps to carry oxygen to the hair follicles

- Green leafy vegetables
- Eggs
- Chicken
- Pork
- beef

Chapter 13
HEALTHY HAIR GROWTH TIPS

Dear Zany Girl,
I would like to adopt a healthy hair growth routine. I find it difficult at times you try to put so many things in order to achieve this. Can you list some things that would help me establish a routine for my hair?

Dear Reader,
Healthy hair should be considered more of a lifestyle rather than routine. If you see it as just a routine then you may miss opportunities for changes. It should flow with the seasonal changes in your life. Just as you would increase and decrease things in your life as you see fit the same consideration should be taken with your hair. So, let's get on board and change the hair world one lifestyle at a time.

Healthy Hair Growth! We all want it. Some even go to great length to do so by doing numerous things to their scalp to stimulate growth. While some of these methods have proven to be effective, we still need to have a healthy hair lifestyle in place for the long run.

Drink plenty of water
We can't say enough about water for our body. You must drink enough water to keep your body hydrated as well as your hair.

What you eat is everything
How about improving your hair and body at the same time! Eating plenty of foods that's essential to your body is important to keep in mind. (see chapter on foods that benefit the hair)

Exercise
Exercising is important for overall heath and that includes the hair.

Sleep, sleep , sleep
Get enough sleep so that your body can rejuvenate , thus keeping stress at bay.

protection against the elements
You must protect your hair from the blazing sun , which could cause sun damaged hair or the raging winds that could break the ends of your hair off or the cold harsh winter months that could cause dry and brittle hair. How do I do all of this? Yes, leave in conditioner for the heat, hats and scarves from

strong winds and moisturizer for the cold.

Massage your scalp

A scalp massage is important for hair growth because it stimulates blood flow to the scalp, thus increasing circulation and allowing nutrients to get to your hair follicles.

Trim when needed

Trimming hair is a must to prevent further breakage up the hair follicle. It keeps the hair strands healthy.

Coloring too often

Coloring too often and result in dry and droopy hair strands. Be mindful how often you color and try to only do your new growth as needed and protect your strand that will not be colored by adding a conditioner .

Clean Hair- Healthy hair

Keeping the scalp free from heavy products and dirt will allow your scalp to breath freely.

Use wide tooth combs

Using wide tooth combs will prevent unwanted breakage of hair strands when detangling.

Protective styles are your friend
These styles will help maintain your strands in styles longer and form breakage of combing.

Vitamins
There are several vitamins to choose from, so just get informed about what you need and be consistent with taking them to see results

Learn to relax
what does relaxing have to do with hair? Well, did you know that stress can lead to hair loss. We all have stress in our lives , but it's identifying the stress factors and learning to manage them and relax our minds. Whatever that thing that you do to relax, whether you watch a movie, cooking, journaling, reading a book, spa day or helping others to help you relax. You may want to try some new things like breathing exercise, going for a walk, sitting at the park reading a book, yoga, Zumba, wine and laughter with good friends.

Chapter 14
SUMMER/ WINTER HAIRCARE

Dear Zany Girl,
I didn't realize that my natural hair would change from season to season and that I would have to change my regimen to prevent and protect my hair. The problem is that I'm not sure what I need to consider for those different seasons. Can you help?

Dear Reader,
Unfortunately, as the seasons change our hair requires a different type of care to protect from heat , cold and prevent breakage and dryness. You should not change your products from winter to summer months, but the manner in which you use them. In the summer months you could easily leave the house with a wash n go and allow it to air dry, however you could not do that in the cold winter months. Same wash n go, but one requires a drying technique while the other is more freestyle.

Seasonal Haircare

Seasonal hair care is important to know so that you can lessen your frustration with your hair. You need to know what your hair needs at all times for it to cooperate with styles. Just as you would change your wardrobe and makeup from season to season , haircare routine would be no difference.

Winter Time Care

The dry and cold winter months will suck the moisture out of your hair and leave it dry, brittle and lifeless.

We can protect our hair with added moisture, then add more moisture. Feel free to slather on the heavier conditioners like shea butter, deep conditioners will prevent damage and condition your hair, while oil treatments will seal the moisture in the hair.

Tips for the colder months
- ❖ protective styles are good for protecting your ends
- ❖ add a bit more deep conditioners and sealants in your care
- ❖ hats and scarves are good for coverage

Summer Time Care

Let's be real! The summer months will leave your hair fighting against humidity, sun damage, and chlorine damage unless you are prepared to protect your strands. You should continue to use your normal products, but change the method in which you use them.

In the warmer weather you may want to lighten up your butter by adding a water based moisturizer to it. You may want to use it more of a sealant rather than for twist out and such. If you put on too many heavy butters the heat will surely melt it and you will have a running mess on your shoulders and neck.

Can you say, oil rinse! They are great for adding moisture to your hair, protecting against the humidity, and even frizz control. Just choose the oils that compliment your need and oil rinse away.

Protective styles are not needed. Time to let your hair out and, enjoy your natural hair and just be free.

Tips for the warmer months
- use lighter oils; and butter to seal hair instead of as styling tool.
- Hats and scarves are good protection
- Freestyles like wash n go, twist out, and braids out
- Use leave in conditioners as sun protection

CHAPTER 15
HAIR CARE TOOLS

Dear Zany Girl,

I often find that I began styling my hair and realize that I need certain items. This is frustrating to me, please list the most important daily essentials tools that I should have on hand at all times for styling my hair.

Dear Reader,

There are tools that every person needs to have regardless of your hair type. So, kick the frustration with not knowing what to do and equip yourself with the right tools at the right time for a good hair day.

Hair clips-These are good for pinning down twist out or doing roller sets. Use them as you see fit.

Afro Pick-
If you need volume and fluff to your twist out or wash n go, then grab an afro pick and lift from the root

Tangle Tweezer-
Awesome for detangling both wet and dry hair along with giving great curl definition.

Spray bottles. This is essential to your morning and night routine.

Rat Tail Comb
When you are in need of a straight part of your style , then you will need a rat tail comb in your bag.

Ouidad Comb
This double comb will cut your detangling session in half.

Hair pins-These are loose pins to use for a not so secure hold. Use as you like for protective styles.

Bobbi pins. These are closed and will have a more secure hold than the hairpin. Use as you like for protective styles.

Wide tooth comb
Great for detangling natural hair

NATURAL HAIR QUESTIONS ANSWERED

Shower brush- use for detangling in the shower

Denman brush-
This brush is great for detangling and a curl definer.

Ouchless ponytail holder- ponytail holder that will not pull or snag your hair

Satin scrunches – use for night time Bunning or pineapple method

Satin pillow case- sleep on this to retain moisture in your hair

Satin head wrap- wrap your hair with this to retain moisture

hand dry hair glove- great for your shortcut or to squeeze some water from hair

Plastic caps- use these for oil treatments and deep conditioners

Microfiber towels- The microfiber fabric will soak up water quickly

Hand held hair steamer- Great for adding moisture to your hair and can take along on travel.

Tips for daily traveling
- ❖ Always carry bobby pins , ponytail holders in your bag. You never know when you need to change your hair style.
- ❖ When staying overnight away from home, remember to bring your satin pillow case.
- ❖ Keep away from home hair bag with all of your essentials and you will never be caught off guard by the change in weather or event.

I have purposely left out hair charts or rubric to measure the type of hair strand that you have. Natural is about being free, not about succumbing to a discriminatory system that categorizes us into a higher or lesser category.

These were created to assist you in learning about your hair. However, when used incorrectly it can add a dividing line between us naturals to use at our disposal to discriminate amongst each other.

If you use this chart, do so to be informed about your hair type so that you can choose products accordingly for hair. I have witnessed people saying "Oh … I wish I was that hair type" while diminishing their own hair type." That is not what it is for.

Just be natural and be free.

ABOUT THE AUTHOR

Tambeara Watkins was born and raised in Atlanta Georgia. She enjoys outdoor hiking, music to soothe her soul, food that captures her attention, designing with a purpose, drinking morning cups of coffee, juicing for health, exercising for life, and writing to express herself in wisdom and love. She hopes that others would find their peace and life's journey.

ZANY GIRL
NATURAL HAIR QUESTIONS ANSWERED

www.ingramcontent.com/pod-product-compliance
Lightning Source LLC
Chambersburg PA
CBHW070547300426
44113CB00011B/1816